GEORGE HERBERT Poems selected by JO SHAPCOTT

George Herbert (1593–1633) was educated at Westminster School and Trinity College, Cambridge, where he was appointed Reader in Rhetoric in 1618 and Public Orator in 1620. He was a Greek and Latin scholar, was fluent in modern languages and an accomplished musician. In 1626 he resigned his seat in parliament and took holy orders, becoming Rector of Bemerton, a tiny rural parish on Salisbury Plain, in 1630. *The Temple*, Herbert's great structure of poems from which the present selection is drawn, first appeared in 1633, the year of his death.

Jo Shapcott was born in London. Poems from her three award-winning collections *Electroplating the Baby*, *Phrase Book* and *My Life Asleep* are gathered in *Her Book: Poems 1988–1998*. She has won a number of literary prizes including the Commonwealth Prize for Best First Collection, the Forward Prize for Best Collection and the National Poetry Competition (twice). Her most recent collection is *Tender Taxes*, versions of Rilke's French poems (Faber, 2001), and she is the co-editor of *Emergency Kit* (Faber, 1996).

IN THE POET-TO-POET SERIES

GEORGE HERBERT
Poems selected by JO SHAPCOTT

Introduction by W. H. AUDEN

faber and faber

First published in 2006
by Faber and Faber Limited
3 Queen Square London WC1N 3AU

Photoset by RefineCatch Ltd, Bungay, Suffolk
Printed in England by Bookmarque Ltd, Croydon, Surrey

A CIP record for this book
is available from the British Library

ISBN 978–0–571–21039–8
      0–571–21039–2

10 9 8 7 6 5 4 3 2 1

Contents

Introduction

Reading a poet whose work I admire, it is only very seldom that I find myself wishing: 'Oh, how I would like to have been an intimate friend of his!' There are some, like Byron, whom I would like to have met once, but most, I feel, would either, like Dante and Goethe, have been too intimidating, or, like Wordsworth, too disagreeable. The two English poets, neither of them, perhaps, major poets, whom I would most like to have known well are William Barnes and George Herbert.

Even if Issak Walton had never written his life, I think that any reader of his poetry will conclude that George Herbert must have been an exceptionally good man, and exceptionally nice as well.

He was born in Montgomery Castle on 3 April 1593, the fifth son of Sir Richard Herbert and Lady Magdalen Herbert, to whom Donne dedicated his elegy 'Autumnal Beauty', and his uncle was Lord Herbert of Cherbury. By birth, that is to say, he enjoyed a secure social position. In addition Nature had endowed him with the gifts of intelligence and personal charm. Educated at Westminster School and Trinity College, Cambridge, he became a Fellow of the latter in 1616, and was appointed Public Orator to the University in 1620. He was not only an excellent Greek and Latin scholar, but also fluent in Italian, Spanish and French, and an accomplished amateur musician who played the lute and composed songs.

For a young man of his breeding and talents one would have prophesied a great future in the world. He soon attracted the attention of two powerful and influential figures, the Duke of Richmond and the Marquess of Hamilton and, when they met, King James I took great fancy to him.

His own ambition was as great as his opportunities. He seems to have dreamed of one day becoming a Secretary of State and this led him somewhat to neglect his duties as Public Orator in order to attend the Court. The Academic Life, evidently, was not altogether to his taste. Walton tells us:

... he had often designed to leave the university, and decline all study, which he thought did impair his health; for he had a body apt to a consumption, and to fevers, and other infirmities, which he judged were increased by his studies ... But his mother would by no means allow him to leave the university or to travel; and though he inclined very much to both, yet he would by no means satisfy his own desires at so dear a rate as to prove an undutiful son to so affectionate a mother.

This is confirmed in the poem 'Affliction':

> Whereas my birth and spirit rather took
> > The way that takes the town;
> Thou didst betray me to a lingring book,
> > And wrap me in a gown.
> I was entangled in the world of strife,
> Before I had the power to change my life.
>
> Yet, for I threatned oft the siege to raise,
> > Not simpring all mine age,
> Thou often didst with Academick praise
> > Melt and dissolve my rage.
> I took thy sweetned pill, till I came where
> I could not go away, nor persevere.

Though he writes in another poem, 'The Pearl':

> I know the wages of Pleasure, the sweet strains,
> The lullings and the relishes of it;
> The propositions of hot bloud and brains;

one does not get the impression from his work that the temptations of the flesh were a serious spiritual menace to him, as they were to Donne. Nor did he suffer from religious doubts: in the seventeenth century very few people did. His struggle was with worldliness, the desire to move in high circles, to enjoy fame and power, and to such temptations he might very well have succumbed, had not his two aristocratic patrons and then, in 1625, King James, all died, thus dashing his hopes of immediate preferment.

For the first time he began to consider seriously the possibility of taking Holy Orders, a course which his mother had always prayed for. Most of his friends disagreed, thinking the priesthood too mean an employment, too much below his birth and natural abilities. To one such counsellor, he replied:

It hath been formerly adjudged that the domestic servants of the King of heaven should be of the noblest families on earth; and though the iniquity of the late times have made clergymen meanly valued, and the sacred name of priest contemptible, yet I will labour to make it honorable by consecrating all my learning, and all my poor abilities, to advance the glory of that God that gave them.

These words show that Herbert was under no illusion as to the sacrifice he would have to make, and to come to a definite decision was clearly a struggle, for he was not ordained a priest until 1630 when he was made Rector of Bemerton, a tiny rural parish on Salisbury Plain. In the previous year he had married Jane Danvers after a courtship of only three days, and the marriage turned out to be a very happy one. In 1633 he died of consumption at the age of only forty.

Since none of his poems were published during his lifetime, we cannot say for certain when any of them were written, but one suspects that it was from the two and a half years of indecision that many of them, particularly those which deal with temptations and feelings of rebellion, must date.

Since all of Herbert's poems are concerned with the religious life, they cannot be judged by aesthetic standards alone. His poetry is the counterpart of Jeremy Taylor's prose: together they are the finest expressions we have of Anglican piety at its best. Donne, though an Anglican, is, both in his poems and his sermons, much too much of a *prima donna* to be typical.

Comparing the Anglican Church with the Roman Catholic Church on the one hand and the Calvinist on the other, Herbert writes:

A fine aspect in fit gray,
Neither too mean, nor yet too gay,
         Shows who is best.
Outlandish looks may not compare:
For all they either painted are,
         Or else undrest.

She on the hills, which wantonly
Allureth all in hope to be
         By her preferr'd,
Hath kiss'd so long her painted shrines,
That ev'n her face by kissing shines,
         For her reward.

She in the valley is so shie
Of dressing, that her hair doth lie
         About her eares:
While she avoids her neighbours pride,
She wholly goes on th' other side,
         And nothing wears.

Herbert, it will he noticed, says nothing about differences in theological dogma. The Anglican Church has always avoided strict dogmatic definitions. The Thirty-Nine Articles, for example, can be interpreted either in a Calvinist or a non-Calvinist sense, and her Office of Holy Communion can be accepted both by Zwinglians who regard it as a service of Commemoration only, and by those who believe in the Real Presence. Herbert is concerned with liturgical manners and styles of piety. In his day, Catholic piety was typically baroque, both in architecture and in poets like Crashaw. This was too unrestrained for his taste. On the other hand, he found the style of worship practised by the Reformed Churches too severe, too 'inward'. He would have agreed with Launcelot Andrewes who said: 'If we worship God with our hearts only and not also with our hats, something is lacking.' The Reformers, for instance, disapproved of all religious images, but Herbert thought that, on occasions, a stained-glass window could be of more spiritual help than a sermon.

> Doctrine and life, colours and light, in one
> > When they combine and mingle, bring
> A strong regard and aw; but speech alone
> > Doth vanish like a flaring thing,
> > And in the eare, not conscience ring.

Walton tells us that he took enormous pains to explain to his parishioners, most of whom were probably illiterate, the significance of every ritual act in the liturgy, and to instruct them in the meaning of the Church Calendar. He was not a mystic like Vaughan: few Anglicans have been. One might almost say that Anglican piety at its best, as represented by Herbert, is the piety of a gentleman, which means, of course, that at its second best it becomes merely genteel.

As a Christian, he realized that his own style of poetry had its spiritual dangers:

> . . . Is there in truth no beautie?
> Is all good structure in a winding stair?

But as a poet he knew that he must be true to his sensibility, that all he could do was to wash his sweet phrases and lovely metaphors with his tears and bring them

> to church well drest and clad:
> My God must have my best, even all I had.

He is capable of writing lines of a Dante-esque directness. For example:

> Man stole the fruit, but I must climb the tree,
> The Tree of Life to all but only Me.

But as a rule he is more ingenious, though never, I think, obscure.

Each thing is fully of dutie:
Waters united are our navigation;
Distinguished, our habitation;
Below, our drink; above, our meat;
Both are our cleanlinesse. Hath one such beautie?
Then how are all things neat?

He is capable of clever antitheses which remind one of Pope, as when, speaking of a woman's love of pearls for which some diver has risked his life, he says:

Who with excessive pride
Her own destruction and his danger wears.

And in a most remarkable sonnet, 'Prayer', he seems to foreshadow Mallarmé.

Church-bels beyond the starres heard, the souls bloud,
The land of spices; something understood.

Wit he had in abundance. Take, for example, 'The Church-Porch'. Its subject matter is a series of moral maxims about social behaviour. One expects to be utterly bored but, thanks to Herbert's wit, one is entertained. Thus, he takes the commonplace maxim, 'Don't monopolize the conversation', and turns it into:

If thou be Master-gunner, spend not all
That thou canst speak, at once; but husband it,
And give men turns of speech: do not forestall
By lavishnesse thine own, and others wit,
    As if thou mad'st thy will. A civil guest
    Will no more talk all, then eat all the feast.

A good example of his technical skill is the poem 'Denial'. He was, as we know, a skilled musician, and I am sure he got the idea for the structure of this poem from his musical experience of discords and resolving them. The first five stanzas consist of a quatrain, rhymed *abab*, followed by a line which comes as a shock because it does not rhyme:

O that thou shouldst give dust a tongue
                    To crie to thee,
And then not heare it crying! all day long
                    My heart was in my knee,
                                But no hearing.

But in the final stanza the discord is resolved with a rhyme.

O cheer and tune my heartlesse breast,
                    Deferre no time;
That so thy favours granting my request,
                    They and my minde may chime,
                                And mend my ryme.

This poem and many others also show Herbert's gift for securing musical effects by varying the length of the lines in a stanza. Of all the so-called 'metaphysical' poets he has the subtlest ear. As George Macdonald said of him:

> The music of a poem is its meaning in sound as distinguished from word . . . The sound of a verse is the harbinger of the truth contained in it . . . Herein Herbert excels. It will be found impossible to separate the music of his words from the music of the thought which takes shape in their sound.

And this was Coleridge's estimate:

> George Herbert is a true poet, but a poet *sui generis*, the merits of whose poems will never be felt without a sympathy with the mind and character of the man.

My own sympathy is unbounded.

W. H. AUDEN

GEORGE HERBERT

The Altar

A broken ALTAR, Lord, thy servant reares,
Made of a heart, and cemented with teares:
  Whose parts are as thy hand did frame;
  No workmans tool hath touch'd the same.
        A HEART alone
        Is such a stone,
        As   nothing but
        Thy pow'r doth cut.
        Wherefore each part
        Of my hard heart
        Meets in this frame,
        To praise thy Name:
  That, if I chance to hold my peace,
  These stones to praise thee may not cease.
O let thy blessed SACRIFICE be mine,
And sanctifie this ALTAR to be thine.

The Sinner

Lord, how I am all ague, when I seek
  What I have treasur'd in my memorie!
  Since, if my soul make even with the week,
Each seventh note by right is due to thee.
I finde there quarries of pil'd vanities,
  But shreds of holinesse, that dare not venture
  To shew their face, since crosse to thy decrees:
There the circumference earth is, heav'n the centre.
In so much dregs the quintessence is small:
  The spirit and good extract of my heart
  Comes to about the many hundred part.
Yet Lord restore thine image, heare my call:
  And though my hard heart scarce to thee can grone,
  Remember that thou once didst write in stone.

Redemption

Having been tenant long to a rich Lord,
  Not thriving, I resolved to be bold,
  And make a suit unto him, to afford
A new small-rented lease, and cancell th' old.
In heaven at his manour I him sought:
  They told me there, that he was lately gone
  About some land, which he had dearly bought
Long since on earth, to take possession.
I straight return'd, and knowing his great birth,
  Sought him accordingly in great resorts;
  In cities, theatres, gardens, parks, and courts:
At length I heard a ragged noise and mirth
  Of theeves and murderers: there I him espied,
  Who straight, *Your suit is granted*, said, & died.

Easter

Rise heart; thy Lord is risen. Sing his praise
                        Without delayes,
Who takes thee by the hand, that thou likewise
                        With him mayst rise:
That, as his death calcined thee to dust,
His life may make thee gold, and much more, just.

Awake, my lute, and struggle for thy part
                        With all thy art.
The crosse taught all wood to resound his name,
                        Who bore the same.
His stretched sinews taught all strings, what key
Is best to celebrate this most high day.

Consort both heart and lute, and twist a song
                        Pleasant and long:
Or, since all musick is but three parts vied
                        And multiplied,
O let thy blessed Spirit bear a part,
And make up our defects with his sweet art.

    I got me flowers to straw thy way;
    I got me boughs off many a tree:
    But thou wast up by break of day,
    And brought'st thy sweets along with thee.

    The Sunne arising in the East,
    Though he give light, & th' East perfume;
    If they should offer to contest
    With thy arising, they presume.

    Can there be any day but this,
    Though many sunnes to shine endeavour?
    We count three hundred, but we misse:
    There is but one, and that one ever.

Easter-wings

Lord, who createdst man in wealth and store,
   Though foolishly he lost the same,
      Decaying more and more,
         Till he became
           Most poore:
           With thee
          O let me rise
        As larks, harmoniously,
     And sing this day thy victories:
Then shall the fall further the flight in me.

My tender age in sorrow did beginne:
   And still with sicknesses and shame
      Thou didst so punish sinne,
         That I became
           Most thinne.
           With thee
          Let me combine
        And feel this day thy victorie:
     For, if I imp my wing on thine,
Affliction shall advance the flight in me.

H. Baptisme (II)

Since, Lord, to thee
A narrow way and little gate
Is all the passage, on my infancie
Thou didst lay hold, and antedate
My faith in me.

O let me still
Write thee great God, and me a childe:
Let me be soft and supple to thy will,
Small to my self, to others milde,
Behither ill.

Although by stealth
My flesh get on, yet let her sister
My soul bid nothing, but preserve her wealth:
The growth of flesh is but a blister;
Childhood is health.

Nature

Full of rebellion, I would die,
Or fight, or travell, or denie
That thou hast ought to do with me.
                              O tame my heart;
                    It is thy highest art
To captivate strong holds to thee.

If thou shalt let this venome lurk,
And in suggestions fume and work,
My soul will turn to bubbles straight,
                              And thence by kinde
                    Vanish into a winde,
Making thy workmanship deceit.

O smooth my rugged heart, and there
Engrave thy rev'rend Law and fear;
Or make a new one, since the old
                              Is saplesse grown,
                    And a much fitter stone
To hide my dust, then thee to hold.

Affliction (I)

When first thou didst entice to thee my heart,
                I thought the service brave:
So many joyes I writ down for my part,
                Besides what I might have
Out of my stock of naturall delights,
Augmented with thy gracious benefits.

I looked on thy furniture so fine,
                And made it fine to me:
Thy glorious houshold-stuffe did me entwine,
                And 'tice me unto thee.
Such starres I counted mine: both heav'n and earth
Payd me my wages in a world of mirth.

What pleasures could I want, whose King I served,
                Where joyes my fellows were?
Thus argu'd into hopes, my thoughts reserved
                No place for grief or fear.
Therefore my sudden soul caught at the place,
And made her youth and fiercenesse seek thy face.

At first thou gav'st me milk and sweetnesses;
                I had my wish and way:
My dayes were straw'd with flow'rs and happinesse;
                There was no moneth but May.
But with my yeares sorrow did twist and grow,
And made a partie unawares for wo.

My flesh began unto my soul in pain,
                Sicknesses cleave my bones;
Consuming agues dwell in ev'ry vein,
                And tune my breath to grones.
Sorrow was all my soul; I scarce beleeved,
Till grief did tell me roundly, that I lived.

When I got health, thou took'st away my life,
                    And more; for my friends die:
My mirth and edge was lost; a blunted knife
                    Was of more use then I.
Thus thinne and lean without a fence or friend,
I was blown through with ev'ry storm and winde.

Whereas my birth and spirit rather took
                    The way that takes the town;
Thou didst betray me to a lingring book,
                    And wrap me in a gown.
I was entangled in the world of strife,
Before I had the power to change my life.

Yet, for I threatned oft the siege to raise,
                    Not simpring all mine age,
Thou often didst with Academick praise
                    Melt and dissolve my rage.
I took thy sweetned pill, till I came where
I could not go away, nor persevere.

Yet lest perchance I should too happie be
                    In my unhappinesse,
Turning my purge to food, thou throwest me
                    Into more sicknesses.
Thus doth thy power crosse-bias me, not making
Thine own gift good, yet me from my wayes taking.

Now I am here, what thou wilt do with me
                    None of my books will show:
I reade, and sigh, and wish I were a tree;
                    For sure then I should grow
To fruit or shade: at least some bird would trust
Her houshold to me, and I should be just.

Yet, though thou troublest me, I must be meek;
                    In weaknesse must be stout.
Well, I will change the service, and go seek

Some other master out.
Ah my deare God! though I am clean forgot,
Let me not love thee, if I love thee not.

Repentance

Lord, I confesse my sinne is great;
    Great is my sinne. Oh! gently treat
With thy quick flow'r, thy momentarie bloom;
                    Whose life still pressing
                    Is one undressing,
    A steadie aiming at a tombe.

Mans age is two houres work, or three:
    Each day doth round about us see.
Thus are we to delights: but we are all
                    To sorrows old,
                    If life be told
    From what life feeleth, Adams fall.

O let thy height of mercie then
    Compassionate short-breathed men.
Cut me not off for my most foul transgression:
                    I do confesse
                    My foolishnesse;
    My God, accept of my confession.

Sweeten at length this bitter bowl,
    Which thou hast pour'd into my soul;
Thy wormwood turn to health, windes to fair weather:
                    For if thou stay,
                    I and this day,
    As we did rise, we die together.

When thou for sinne rebukest man,
    Forthwith he waxeth wo and wan:
Bitternesse fills our bowels; all our hearts
                    Pine, and decay,
                    And drop away,
    And carrie with them th' other parts.

But thou wilt sinne and grief destroy;
That so the broken bones may joy,
And tune together in a well-set song,
                    Full of his praises,
                    Who dead men raises.
Fractures well cur'd make us more strong.

Prayer (I)

Prayer the Churches banquet, Angels age,
   Gods breath in man returning to his birth,
   The soul in paraphrase, heart in pilgrimage,
The Christian plummet sounding heav'n and earth;
Engine against th' Almightie, sinners towre,
   Reversed thunder, Christ-side-piercing spear,
   The six-daies world transposing in an houre,
A kinde of tune, which all things heare and fear;
Softnesse, and peace, and joy, and love, and blisse,
   Exalted Manna, gladnesse of the best,
   Heaven in ordinarie, man well drest,
The milkie way, the bird of Paradise,
   Church-bels beyond the starres heard, the souls bloud,
   The land of spices; something understood.

Antiphon (I)

Cho. Let all the world in ev'ry corner sing,
                                      My God and King.

  Vers. The heav'ns are not too high,
          His praise may thither flie:
          The earth is not too low,
          His praises there may grow.

Cho. Let all the world in ev'ry corner sing,
                                      My God and King.

  Vers. The church with psalms must shout,
          No doore can keep them out:
          But above all, the heart
          Must bear the longest part.

Cho. Let all the world in ev'ry corner sing,
                                      My God and King.

Love (I)

Immortall Love, authour of this great frame,
    Sprung from that beautie which can never fade;
    How hath man parcel'd out thy glorious name,
And thrown it on that dust which thou hast made,
While mortall love doth all the title gain!
    Which siding with invention, they together
    Bear all the sway, possessing heart and brain,
(Thy workmanship) and give thee share in neither.
Wit fancies beautie, beautie raiseth wit:
    The world is theirs; they two play out the game,
    Thou standing by: and though thy glorious name
Wrought our deliverance from th' infernall pit,
    Who sings thy praise? onely a skarf or glove
    Doth warm our hands, and make them write of love.

The Temper (I)

How should I praise thee, Lord! how should my rymes
   Gladly engrave thy love in steel,
  If what my soul doth feel sometimes,
    My soul might ever feel!

Although there were some fourtie heav'ns, or more,
   Sometimes I peere above them all;
  Sometimes I hardly reach a score,
    Sometimes to hell I fall.

O rack me not to such a vast extent;
   Those distances belong to thee:
  The world's too little for thy tent,
    A grave too big for me.

Wilt thou meet arms with man, that thou dost stretch
   A crumme of dust from heav'n to hell?
  Will great God measure with a wretch?
    Shall he thy stature spell?

O let me, when thy roof my soul hath hid,
   O let me roost and nestle there:
  Then of a sinner thou art rid,
    And I of hope and fear.

Yet take thy way; for sure thy way is best:
   Stretch or contract me, thy poore debter:
  This is but tuning of my breast,
    To make the musick better.

Whether I flie with angels, fall with dust,
   Thy hands made both, and I am there:
  Thy power and love, my love and trust
    Make one place ev'ry where.

Employment (I)

If as a flowre doth spread and die,
   Thou wouldst extend me to some good,
Before I were by frosts extremitie
                       Nipt in the bud;

The sweetnesse and the praise were thine;
   But the extension and the room,
Which in thy garland I should fill, were mine
                       At thy great doom.

For as thou dost impart thy grace,
   The greater shall our glorie be.
The measure of our joyes is in this place,
                       The stuffe with thee.

Let me not languish then, and spend
   A life as barren to thy praise,
As is the dust, to which that life doth tend,
                       But with delaies.

All things are busie; onely I
   Neither bring hony with the bees,
Nor flowres to make that, nor the husbandrie
                       To water these.

I am no link of thy great chain,
   But all my companie is a weed.
Lord place me in thy consort; give one strain
                       To my poore reed.

Grace

My stock lies dead, and no increase
Doth my dull husbandrie improve:
O let thy graces without cease
                        Drop from above!

If still the sunne should hide his face,
Thy house would but a dungeon prove,
Thy works nights captives: O let grace
                        Drop from above!

The dew doth ev'ry morning fall;
And shall the dew out-strip thy Dove?
The dew, for which grasse cannot call,
                        Drop from above.

Death is still working like a mole,
And digs my grave at each remove:
Let grace work too, and on my soul
                        Drop from above.

Sinne is still hammering my heart
Unto a hardnesse, void of love:
Let suppling grace, to crosse his art,
                        Drop from above.

O come! for thou dost know the way:
Or if to me thou wilt not move,
Remove me, where I need not say,
                        Drop from above.

Mattens

I cannot ope mine eyes,
    But thou art ready there to catch
  My morning-soul and sacrifice:
Then we must needs for that day make a match.

My God, what is a heart?
  Silver, or gold, or precious stone,
  Or starre, or rainbow, or a part
Of all these things, or all of them in one?

My God, what is a heart,
  That thou shouldst it so eye, and wooe,
  Powring upon it all thy art,
As if that thou hadst nothing els to do?

Indeed mans whole estate
  Amounts (and richly) to serve thee:
  He did not heav'n and earth create,
Yet studies them, not him by whom they be.

Teach me thy love to know;
  That this new light, which now I see,
  May both the work and workman show:
Then by a sunne-beam I will climbe to thee.

Church-monuments

While that my soul repairs to her devotion,
Here I intombe my flesh, that it betimes
May take acquaintance of this heap of dust;
To which the blast of deaths incessant motion,
Fed with the exhalation of our crimes,
Drives all at last. Therefore I gladly trust

My bodie to this school, that it may learn
To spell his elements, and finde his birth
Written in dustie heraldrie and lines;
Which dissolution sure doth best discern,
Comparing dust with dust, and earth with earth.
These laugh at Jeat and Marble put for signes,

To sever the good fellowship of dust,
And spoil the meeting. What shall point out them,
When they shall bow, and kneel, and fall down flat
To kisse those heaps, which now they have in trust?
Deare flesh, while I do pray, learn here thy stemme
And true descent; that when thou shalt grow fat,

And wanton in thy cravings, thou mayst know,
That flesh is but the glasse, which holds the dust
That measures all our time; which also shall
Be crumbled into dust. Mark here below
How tame these ashes are, how free from lust,
That thou mayst fit thy self against thy fall.

Church-lock and Key

I know it is my sinne, which locks thine eares,
                              And bindes thy hands,
Out-crying my requests, drowning my tears;
Or else the chilnesse of my faint demands.

But as cold hands are angrie with the fire,
                              And mend it still;
So I do lay the want of my desire,
Not on my sinnes, or coldnesse, but thy will.

Yet heare, O God, onely for his blouds sake
                              Which pleads for me:
For though sinnes plead too, yet like stones they make
His blouds sweet current much more loud to be.

The Church-floore

Mark you the floore? that square & speckled stone,
  Which looks so firm and strong,
    Is *Patience*:

And th' other black and grave, wherewith each one
  Is checker'd all along,
    Humilitie:

The gentle rising, which on either hand
  Leads to the Quire above,
    Is *Confidence*:

But the sweet cement, which in one sure band
  Ties the whole frame, is *Love*
    And *Charitie*.

  Hither sometimes Sinne steals, and stains
  The marbles neat and curious veins:
But all is cleansed when the marble weeps.
  Sometimes Death, puffing at the doore,
  Blows all the dust about the floore:
But while he thinks to spoil the room, he sweeps.
  Blest be the *Architect*, whose art
  Could build so strong in a weak heart.

The Windows

Lord, how can man preach thy eternall word?
        He is a brittle crazie glasse:
Yet in thy temple thou dost him afford
        This glorious and transcendent place,
        To be a window, through thy grace.

But when thou dost anneal in glasse thy storie,
        Making thy life to shine within
The holy Preachers; then the light and glorie
        More rev'rend grows, & more doth win:
        Which else shows watrish, bleak, & thin.

Doctrine and life, colours and light, in one
        When they combine and mingle, bring
A strong regard and aw: but speech alone
        Doth vanish like a flaring thing,
        And in the eare, not conscience ring.

Content

Peace mutt'ring thoughts, and do not grudge to keep
      Within the walls of your own breast:
Who cannot on his own bed sweetly sleep,
      Can on anothers hardly rest.

Gad not abroad at ev'ry quest and call
      Of an untrained hope or passion.
To court each place or fortune that doth fall,
      Is wantonnesse in contemplation.

Mark how the fire in flints doth quiet lie,
      Content and warm t' it self alone:
But when it would appeare to others eye,
      Without a knock it never shone.

Give me the pliant minde, whose gentle measure
      Complies and suits with all estates;
Which can let loose to a crown, and yet with pleasure
      Take up within a cloisters gates.

This soul doth span the world, and hang content
      From either pole unto the centre:
Where in each room of the well-furnisht tent
      He lies warm, and without adventure.

The brags of life are but a nine dayes wonder;
      And after death the fumes that spring
From private bodies make as big a thunder,
      As those which rise from a huge King.

Onely thy Chronicle is lost; and yet
      Better by worms be all once spent,
Then to have hellish moths still gnaw and fret
      Thy name in books, which may not rent:

When all thy deeds, whose brunt thou feel'st alone,
      Are chaw'd by others pens and tongue;
And as their wit is, their digestion,
      Thy nourisht fame is weak or strong.

Then cease discoursing soul, till thine own ground,
      Do not thy self or friends importune.
He that by seeking hath himself once found,
      Hath ever found a happie fortune.

The Quidditie

My God, a verse is not a crown,
No point of honour, or gay suit,
No hawk, or banquet, or renown,
Nor a good sword, nor yet a lute:

It cannot vault, or dance, or play;
It never was in *France* or *Spain*;
Nor can it entertain the day
With my great stable or demain:

It is no office, art, or news,
Nor the Exchange, or busie Hall;
But it is that which while I use
I am with thee, and *most take all*.

Humilitie

I saw the Vertues sitting hand in hand
In sev'rall ranks upon an azure throne,
Where all the beasts and fowl by their command
Presented tokens of submission.
Humilitie, who sat the lowest there
                  To execute their call,
When by the beasts the presents tendred were,
                  Gave them about to all.

The angrie Lion did present his paw,
Which by consent was giv'n to Mansuetude.
The fearfull Hare her eares, which by their law
Humilitie did reach to Fortitude.
The jealous Turkie brought his corall-chain;
                  That went to Temperance.
On Justice was bestow'd the Foxes brain,
                  Kill'd in the way by chance.

At length the Crow bringing the Peacocks plume,
(For he would not) as they beheld the grace
Of that brave gift, each one began to fume,
And challenge it, as proper to his place,
Till they fell out: which when the beasts espied,
                  They leapt upon the throne;
And if the Fox had liv'd to rule their side,
                  They had depos'd each one.

Humilitie, who held the plume, at this
Did weep so fast, that the tears trickling down
Spoil'd all the train: then saying, *Here it is*
For which ye wrangle, made them turn their frown
Against the beasts: so joyntly bandying,
                  They drive them soon away;
And then amerc'd them, double gifts to bring
                  At the next Session-day.

Constancie

Who is the honest man?
    He that doth still and strongly good pursue,
To God, his neighbour, and himself most true:
    Whom neither force nor fawning can
Unpinne, or wrench from giving all their due.

    Whose honestie is not
So loose or easie, that a ruffling winde
Can blow away, or glittering look it blinde:
    Who rides his sure and even trot,
While the world now rides by, now lags behinde.

    Who, when great trials come,
Nor seeks, nor shunnes them; but doth calmly stay,
Till he the thing and the example weigh:
    All being brought into a summe,
What place or person calls for, he doth pay.

    Whom none can work or wooe
To use in any thing a trick or sleight;
For above all things he abhorres deceit:
    His words and works and fashion too
All of a piece, and all are cleare and straight.

    Who never melts or thaws
At close tentations: when the day is done,
His goodnesse sets not, but in dark can runne:
    The sunne to others writeth laws,
And is their vertue; Vertue is his Sunne.

    Who, when he is to treat
With sick folks, women, those whom passions sway,
Allows for that, and keeps his constant way:
    Whom others faults do not defeat;
But though men fail him, yet his part doth play.

        Whom nothing can procure,
When the wide world runnes bias from his will,
To writhe his limbes, and share, not mend the ill.
        This is the Mark-man, safe and sure,
Who still is right, and prayes to be so still.

The Starre

Bright spark, shot from a brighter place,
    Where beams surround my Saviours face,
        Canst thou be any where
           So well as there?

Yet, if thou wilt from thence depart,
    Take a bad lodging in my heart;
        For thou canst make a debter,
           And make it better.

First with thy fire-work burn to dust
    Folly, and worse then folly, lust:
        Then with thy light refine,
           And make it shine:

So disengag'd from sinne and sicknesse,
    Touch it with thy celestiall quicknesse,
        That it may hang and move
           After thy love.

Then with our trinitie of light,
    Motion, and heat, let's take our flight
        Unto the place where thou
           Before didst bow.

Get me a standing there, and place
    Among the beams, which crown the face
        Of him, who dy'd to part
           Sinne and my heart:

That so among the rest I may
    Glitter, and curle, and winde as they:
        That winding is their fashion
           Of adoration.

Sure thou wilt joy, by gaining me
To flie home like a laden bee
Unto that hive of beams
And garland-streams.

Employment (II)

He that is weary, let him sit.
    My soul would stirre
And trade in courtesies and wit,
    Quitting the furre
To cold complexions needing it.
Man is no starre, but a quick coal
    Of mortall fire:
Who blows it not, nor doth controll
    A faint desire,
Lets his own ashes choke his soul.
When th' elements did for place contest
    With him, whose will
Ordain'd the highest to be best;
    The earth sat still,
And by the others is opprest.
Life is a businesse, not good cheer;
    Ever in warres.
The sunne still shineth there or here,
    Whereas the starres
Watch an advantage to appeare.
Oh that I were an Orenge-tree,
    That busie plant!
Then should I ever laden be,
    And never want
Some fruit for him that dressed me.
But we are still too young or old;
    The Man is gone,
Before we do our wares unfold:
    So we freeze on,
Untill the grave increase our cold.

Deniall

When my devotions could not pierce
           Thy silent eares;
Then was my heart broken, as was my verse:
        My breast was full of fears
           And disorder:

My bent thoughts, like a brittle bow,
           Did flie asunder:
Each took his way; some would to pleasures go,
        Some to the warres and thunder
           Of alarms.

As good go any where, they say,
           As to benumme
Both knees and heart, in crying night and day,
        Come, come, my God, O come,
           But no hearing.

O that thou shouldst give dust a tongue
           To crie to thee,
And then not heare it crying! all day long
        My heart was in my knee,
           But no hearing.

Therefore my soul lay out of sight,
           Untun'd, unstrung:
My feeble spirit, unable to look right,
        Like a nipt blossome, hung
           Discontented.

O cheer and tune my heartlesse breast,
           Deferre no time;
That so thy favours granting my request,
        They and my minde may chime,
           And mend my ryme.

Sighs and Grones

O do not use me
After my sinnes! look not on my desert,
But on thy glorie! then thou wilt reform
And not refuse me: for thou onely art
The mightie God, but I a sillie worm;
O do not bruise me!

O do not urge me!
For what account can thy ill steward make?
I have abus'd thy stock, destroy'd thy woods,
Suckt all thy magazens: my head did ake,
Till it found out how to consume thy goods:
O do not scourge me!

O do not blinde me!
I have deserv'd that an Egyptian night
Should thicken all my powers; because my lust
Hath still sow'd fig-leaves to exclude thy light:
But I am frailtie, and already dust;
O do not grinde me!

O do not fill me
With the turn'd viall of thy bitter wrath!
For thou hast other vessels full of bloud,
A part whereof my Saviour empti'd hath,
Ev'n unto death: since he di'd for my good,
O do not kill me!

But O reprieve me!
For thou hast *life* and *death* at thy command;
Thou art both *Judge* and *Saviour*, *feast* and *rod*,
Cordiall and *Corrosive*: put not thy hand
Into the bitter box; but O my God,
My God, relieve me!

The World

Love built a stately house; where *Fortune* came,
And spinning phansies, she was heard to say,
That her fine cobwebs did support the frame,
Whereas they were supported by the same:
But *Wisdome* quickly swept them all away.

Then *Pleasure* came, who liking not the fashion,
Began to make *Balcones*, *Terraces*,
Till she had weakned all by alteration:
But rev'rend *laws*, and many a *proclamation*
Reformed all at length with menaces.

Then enter'd *Sinne*, and with that Sycomore,
Whose leaves first sheltred man from drought & dew,
Working and winding slily evermore,
The inward walls and sommers cleft and tore:
But *Grace* shor'd these, and cut that as it grew.

Then *Sinne* combin'd with *Death* in a firm band
To raze the building to the very floore:
Which they effected; none could them withstand.
But *Love* and *Grace* took *Glorie* by the hand,
And built a braver Palace then before.

Vanitie (I)

The fleet Astronomer can bore,
And thred the spheres with his quick-piercing minde:
He views their stations, walks from doore to doore,
Surveys, as if he had design'd
To make a purchase there: he sees their dances,
And knoweth long before
Both their full-ey'd aspects, and secret glances.

The nimble Diver with his side
Cuts through the working waves, that he may fetch
His dearely-earned pearl, which God did hide
On purpose from the ventrous wretch;
That he might save his life, and also hers,
Who with excessive pride
Her own destruction and his danger wears.

The subtil Chymick can devest
And strip the creature naked, till he finde
The callow principles within their nest:
There he imparts to them his minde,
Admitted to their bed-chamber, before
They appeare trim and drest
To ordinarie suitours at the doore.

What hath not man sought out and found,
But his deare God? who yet his glorious law
Embosomes in us, mellowing the ground
With showres and frosts, with love & aw,
So that we need not say, Where's this command?
Poore man, thou searchest round
To finde out *death*, but missest *life* at hand.

Vertue

Sweet day, so cool, so calm, so bright,
The bridall of the earth and skie:
The dew shall weep thy fall to night;
                For thou must die.

Sweet rose, whose hue angrie and brave
Bids the rash gazer wipe his eye:
Thy root is ever in its grave,
                And thou must die.

Sweet spring, full of sweet dayes and roses,
A box where sweets compacted lie;
My musick shows ye have your closes,
                And all must die.

Onely a sweet and vertuous soul,
Like season'd timber, never gives;
But though the whole world turn to coal,
                Then chiefly lives.

The Pearl. Matth. 13. 45

I know the wayes of Learning; both the head
And pipes that feed the presse, and make it runne;
What reason hath from nature borrowed,
Or of it self, like a good huswife, spunne
In laws and policie; what the starres conspire,
What willing nature speaks, what forc'd by fire;
Both th' old discoveries, and the new-found seas,
The stock and surplus, cause and historie:
All these stand open, or I have the keyes:
                Yet I love thee.

I know the wayes of Honour, what maintains
The quick returns of courtesie and wit:
In vies of favours whether partie gains,
When glorie swells the heart, and moldeth it
To all expressions both of hand and eye,
Which on the world a true-love-knot may tie,
And bear the bundle, wheresoe're it goes:
How many drammes of spirit there must be
To sell my life unto my friends or foes:
                Yet I love thee.

I know the wayes of Pleasure, the sweet strains,
The lullings and the relishes of it;
The propositions of hot bloud and brains;
What mirth and musick mean; what love and wit
Have done these twentie hundred yeares, and more:
I know the projects of unbridled store:
My stuffe is flesh, not brasse; my senses live,
And grumble oft, that they have more in me
Then he that curbs them, being but one to five:
                Yet I love thee.

I know all these, and have them in my hand:
Therefore not sealed, but with open eyes
I flie to thee, and fully understand
Both the main sale, and the commodities;
And at what rate and price I have thy love;
With all the circumstances that may move:
Yet through these labyrinths, not my groveling wit,
But thy silk twist let down from heav'n to me,
Did both conduct and teach me, how by it
                    To climbe to thee.

Affliction (IV)

Broken in pieces all asunder,
        Lord, hunt me not,
        A thing forgot,
Once a poore creature, now a wonder,
        A wonder tortur'd in the space
        Betwixt this world and that of grace.

My thoughts are all a case of knives,
        Wounding my heart
        With scatter'd smart,
As watring pots give flowers their lives.
        Nothing their furie can controll,
        While they do wound and pink my soul.

All my attendants are at strife,
        Quitting their place
        Unto my face:
Nothing performs the task of life:
        The elements are let loose to fight,
        And while I live, trie out their right.

Oh help, my God! let not their plot
        Kill them and me,
        And also thee,
Who art my life: dissolve the knot,
        As the sunne scatters by his light
        All the rebellions of the night.

Then shall those powers, which work for grief,
        Enter thy pay,
        And day by day
Labour thy praise, and my relief;
        With care and courage building me,
        Till I reach heav'n, and much more, thee.

Man

My God, I heard this day,
That none doth build a stately habitation,
But he that means to dwell therein.
What house more stately hath there been,
Or can be, then is Man? to whose creation
All things are in decay.

For Man is ev'ry thing,
And more: He is a tree, yet bears more fruit;
A beast, yet is, or should be more:
Reason and speech we onely bring.
Parrats may thank us, if they are not mute,
They go upon the score.

Man is all symmetrie,
Full of proportions, one limbe to another,
And all to all the world besides:
Each part may call the furthest, brother:
For head with foot hath private amitie,
And both with moons and tides.

Nothing hath got so farre,
But Man hath caught and kept it, as his prey.
His eyes dismount the highest starre:
He is in little all the sphere.
Herbs gladly cure our flesh; because that they
Finde their acquaintance there.

For us the windes do blow,
The earth doth rest, heav'n move, and fountains flow.
Nothing we see, but means our good,
As our delight, or as our treasure:
The whole is, either our cupboard of food,
Or cabinet of pleasure.

The starres have us to bed;
Night draws the curtain, which the sunne withdraws;
Musick and light attend our head.
All things unto our flesh are kinde
In their descent and being; to our minde
In their ascent and cause.

Each thing is full of dutie:
Waters united are our navigation;
Distinguished, our habitation;
Below, our drink; above, our meat;
Both are our cleanlinesse. Hath one such beautie?
Then how are all things neat?

More servants wait on Man,
Then he'l take notice of: in ev'ry path
He treads down that which doth befriend him,
When sicknesse makes him pale and wan.
Oh mightie love! Man is one world, and hath
Another to attend him.

Since then, my God, thou hast
So brave a Palace built; O dwell in it,
That it may dwell with thee at last!
Till then, afford us so much wit;
That, as the world serves us, we may serve thee,
And both thy servants be.

Life

I made a posie, while the day ran by:
Here will I smell my remnant out, and tie
                My life within this band.
But Time did becken to the flowers, and they
By noon most cunningly did steal away,
                And wither'd in my hand.

My hand was next to them, and then my heart:
I took, without more thinking, in good part
                Times gentle admonition:
Who did so sweetly deaths sad taste convey,
Making my minde to smell my fatall day;
                Yet sugring the suspicion.

Farewell deare flowers, sweetly your time ye spent,
Fit, while ye liv'd, for smell or ornament,
                And after death for cures.
I follow straight without complaints or grief,
Since if my sent be good, I care not if
                It be as short as yours.

Mortification

How soon doth man decay!
      When clothes are taken from a chest of sweets
To swaddle infants, whose young breath
      Scarce knows the way;
Those clouts are little winding sheets,
Which do consigne and send them unto death.

When boyes go first to bed,
They step into their voluntarie graves,
      Sleep bindes them fast; onely their breath
      Makes them not dead:
Successive nights, like rolling waves,
Convey them quickly, who are bound for death.

When youth is frank and free,
And calls for musick, while his veins do swell,
      All day exchanging mirth and breath
      In companie;
That musick summons to the knell,
Which shall befriend him at the houre of death.

When man grows staid and wise,
Getting a house and home, where he may move
      Within the circle of his breath,
      Schooling his eyes;
That dumbe inclosure maketh love
Unto the coffin, that attends his death.

When age grows low and weak,
Marking his grave, and thawing ev'ry yeare,
      Till all do melt, and drown his breath
      When he would speak;
A chair or litter shows the biere,
Which shall convey him to the house of death.

Man, ere he is aware,
Hath put together a solemnitie,
   And drest his herse, while he has breath
         As yet to spare:
      Yet Lord, instruct us so to die,
That all these dyings may be life in death.

Miserie

Lord, let the Angels praise thy name.
Man is a foolish thing, a foolish thing,
   Folly and Sinne play all his game.
His house still burns, and yet he still doth sing,
        Man is but grasse,
        He knows it, fill the glasse.

How canst thou brook his foolishnesse?
Why, he'l not lose a cup of drink for thee:
   Bid him but temper his excesse;
Not he: he knows where he can better be,
        As he will swear,
        Then to serve thee in fear.

What strange pollutions doth he wed,
And make his own? as if none knew but he.
   No man shall beat into his head,
That thou within his curtains drawn canst see:
        They are of cloth,
        Where never yet came moth.

The best of men, turn but thy hand
For one poore minute, stumble at a pinne:
   They would not have their actions scann'd,
Nor any sorrow tell them that they sinne,
        Though it be small,
        And measure not their fall.

They quarrell thee, and would give over
The bargain made to serve thee: but thy love
   Holds them unto it, and doth cover
Their follies with the wing of thy milde Dove,
        Not suff'ring those
        Who would, to be thy foes.

My God, Man cannot praise thy name:
Thou art all brightnesse, perfect puritie;
    The sunne holds down his head for shame,
Dead with eclipses, when we speak of thee:
                How shall infection
                Presume on thy perfection?

As dirtie hands foul all they touch,
And those things most, which are most pure and fine:
    So our clay hearts, ev'n when we crouch
To sing thy praises, make them lesse divine.
                Yet either this,
                Or none, thy portion is.

Man cannot serve thee; let him go,
And serve the swine: there, there is his delight:
    He doth not like this vertue, no;
Give him his dirt to wallow in all night:
                These Preachers make
                His head to shoot and ake.

Oh foolish man! where are thine eyes?
How hast thou lost them in a croud of cares?
    Thou pull'st the rug, and wilt not rise,
No, not to purchase the whole pack of starres:
                There let them shine,
                Thou must go sleep, or dine.

The bird that sees a daintie bowre
Made in the tree, where she was wont to sit,
    Wonders and sings, but not his power
Who made the arbour: this exceeds her wit.
                But Man doth know
                The spring, whence all things flow:

And yet, as though he knew it not,
His knowledge winks, and lets his humours reigne;
    They make his life a constant blot,

And all the bloud of God to run in vain.
              Ah wretch! what verse
                Can thy strange wayes rehearse?

  Indeed at first Man was a treasure,
A box of jewels, shop of rarities,
  A ring, whose posie was, *My pleasure*:
He was a garden in a Paradise:
              Glorie and grace
                Did crown his heart and face.

  But sinne hath fool'd him. Now he is
A lump of flesh, without a foot or wing
  To raise him to a glimpse of blisse:
A sick toss'd vessel, dashing on each thing;
              Nay, his own shelf:
                My God, I mean my self.

Conscience

   Peace pratler, do not lowre:
Not a fair look, but thou dost call it foul:
Not a sweet dish, but thou dost call it sowre:
   Musick to thee doth howl.
 By listning to thy chatting fears
 I have both lost mine eyes and eares.

   Pratler, no more, I say:
My thoughts must work, but like a noiselesse sphere;
Harmonious peace must rock them all the day:
   No room for pratlers there.
 If thou persistest, I will tell thee,
 That I have physick to expell thee.

   And the receit shall be
My Saviours bloud: when ever at his board
I do but taste it, straight it cleanseth me,
   And leaves thee not a word;
 No, not a tooth or nail to scratch,
 And at my actions carp, or catch.

   Yet if thou talkest still,
Besides my physick, know there's some for thee:
Some wood and nails to make a staffe or bill
   For those that trouble me:
 The bloudie crosse of my deare Lord
 Is both my physick and my sword.

Home

Come Lord, my head doth burn, my heart is sick,
   While thou dost ever, ever stay:
Thy long deferrings wound me to the quick,
   My spirit gaspeth night and day.
        O show thy self to me,
        Or take me up to thee!

How canst thou stay, considering the pace
   The bloud did make, which thou didst waste?
When I behold it trickling down thy face,
   I never saw thing make such haste.
        O show thy, &c.

When man was lost, thy pitie lookt about
   To see what help in th' earth or skie:
But there was none; at least no help without:
   The help did in thy bosome lie.
        O show thy, &c.

There lay thy sonne: and must he leave that nest,
   That hive of sweetnesse, to remove
Thraldome from those, who would not at a feast
   Leave one poore apple for thy love?
        O show thy, &c.

He did, he came: O my Redeemer deare,
   After all this canst thou be strange?
So many yeares baptiz'd, and not appeare?
   As if thy love could fail or change.
        O show thy, &c.

Yet if thou stayest still, why must I stay?
   My God, what is this world to me,
This world of wo? hence all ye clouds, away,

Away; I must get up and see.
O show thy, &c.

What is this weary world; this meat and drink,
That chains us by the teeth so fast?
What is this woman-kinde, which I can wink
Into a blacknesse and distaste?
O show thy, &c.

With one small sigh thou gav'st me th' other day
I blasted all the joyes about me:
And scouling on them as they pin'd away,
Now come again, said I, and flout me.
O show thy, &c.

Nothing but drought and dearth, but bush and brake,
Which way so-e're I look, I see.
Some may dream merrily, but when they wake,
They dresse themselves and come to thee.
O show thy, &c.

We talk of harvests; there are no such things,
But when we leave our corn and hay:
There is no fruitful yeare, but that which brings
The last and lov'd, though dreadfull day.
O show thy, &c.

Oh loose this frame, this knot of man untie!
That my free soul may use her wing,
Which now is pinion'd with mortalitie,
As an intangled, hamper'd thing.
O show thy, &c.

What have I left, that I should stay and grone?
The most of me to heav'n is fled:
My thoughts and joyes are all packt up and gone,
And for their old acquaintance plead.
O show thy, &c.

Come dearest Lord, passe not this holy season,
    My flesh and bones and joynts do pray:
And ev'n my verse, when by the ryme and reason
    The word is, *Stay*, sayes ever, *Come*.
            O show thy, &c.

The Quip

The merrie world did on a day
With his train-bands and mates agree
To meet together, where I lay,
And all in sport to geere at me.

First, Beautie crept into a rose,
Which when I pluckt not, Sir, said she,
Tell me, I pray, Whose hands are those?
But thou shalt answer, Lord, for me.

Then Money came, and chinking still,
What tune is this, poore man? said he:
I heard in Musick you had skill.
But thou shalt answer, Lord, for me.

Then came brave Glorie puffing by
In silks that whistled, who but he?
He scarce allow'd me half an eie.
But thou shalt answer, Lord, for me.

Then came quick Wit and Conversation,
And he would needs a comfort be,
And, to be short, make an Oration.
But thou shalt answer, Lord, for me.

Yet when the houre of thy designe
To answer these fine things shall come;
Speak not at large; say, I am thine:
And then they have their answer home.

Dulnesse

Why do I languish thus, drooping and dull,
        As if I were all earth?
O give me quicknesse, that I may with mirth
            Praise thee brim-full!

The wanton lover in a curious strain
        Can praise his fairest fair;
And with quaint metaphors her curled hair
            Curl o're again.

Thou art my lovelinesse, my life, my light,
        Beautie alone to me:
Thy bloudy death and undeserv'd, makes thee
            Pure red and white.

When all perfections as but one appeare,
        That those thy form doth show,
The very dust, where thou dost tread and go,
            Makes beauties here.

Where are my lines then? my approaches? views?
        Where are my window-songs?
Lovers are still pretending, & ev'n wrongs
            Sharpen their Muse:

But I am lost in flesh, whose sugred lyes
        Still mock me, and grow bold:
Sure thou didst put a minde there, if I could
            Finde where it lies.

Lord, cleare thy gift, that with a constant wit
        I may but look towards thee:
Look onely; for to *love* thee, who can be,
            What angel fit?

Providence

O sacred Providence, who from end to end
Strongly and sweetly movest, shall I write,
And not of thee, through whom my fingers bend
To hold my quill? shall they not do thee right?

Of all the creatures both in sea and land
Onely to Man thou hast made known thy wayes,
And put the penne alone into his hand,
And made him Secretarie of thy praise.

Beasts fain would sing; birds dittie to their notes;
Trees would be tuning on their native lute
To thy renown: but all their hands and throats
Are brought to Man, while they are lame and mute.

Man is the worlds high Priest: he doth present
The sacrifice for all; while they below
Unto the service mutter an assent,
Such as springs use that fall, and windes that blow.

He that to praise and laud thee doth refrain,
Doth not refrain unto himself alone,
But robs a thousand who would praise thee fain,
And doth commit a world of sinne in one.

The beasts say, Eat me: but, if beasts must teach,
The tongue is yours to eat, but mine to praise.
The trees say, Pull me: but the hand you stretch,
Is mine to write, as it is yours to raise.

Wherefore, most sacred Spirit, I here present
For me and all my fellows praise to thee:
And just it is that I should pay the rent,
Because the benefit accrues to me.

We all acknowledge both thy power and love
To be exact, transcendent, and divine;
Who dost so strongly and so sweetly move,
While all things have their will, yet none but thine.

For either thy command or thy permission
Lay hands on all: they are thy right and left.
The first puts on with speed and expedition;
The other curbs sinnes stealing pace and theft.

Nothing escapes them both; all must appeare,
And be dispos'd, and dress'd, and tun'd by thee,
Who sweetly temper'st all. If we could heare
Thy skill and art, what musick would it be!

Thou art in small things great, not small in any:
Thy even praise can neither rise, nor fall.
Thou art in all things one, in each thing many:
For thou art infinite in one and all.

Tempests are calm to thee; they know thy hand,
And hold it fast, as children do their fathers,
Which crie and follow. Thou hast made poore sand
Check the proud sea, ev'n when it swells and gathers.

Thy cupboard serves the world: the meat is set,
Where all may reach: no beast but knows his feed.
Birds teach us hawking; fishes have their net:
The great prey on the lesse, they on some weed.

Nothing ingendred doth prevent his meat:
Flies have their table spread, ere they appeare.
Some creatures have in winter what to eat;
Others do sleep, and envie not their cheer.

How finely dost thou times and seasons spin,
And make a twist checker'd with night and day!
Which as it lengthens windes, and windes us in,
As bouls go on, but turning all the way.

Each creature hath a wisdome for his good.
The pigeons feed their tender off-spring, crying,
When they are callow; but withdraw their food
When they are fledge, that need may teach them flying.

Bees work for man; and yet they never bruise
Their masters flower, but leave it, having done,
As fair as ever, and as fit to use;
So both the flower doth stay, and hony run.

Sheep eat the grasse, and dung the ground for more:
Trees after bearing drop their leaves for soil:
Springs vent their streams, and by expense get store:
Clouds cool by heat, and baths by cooling boil.

Who hath the vertue to expresse the rare
And curious vertues both of herbs and stones?
Is there an herb for that? O that thy care
Would show a root, that gives expressions!

And if an herb hath power, what have the starres?
A rose, besides his beautie, is a cure.
Doubtlesse our plagues and plentie, peace and warres
Are there much surer then our art is sure.

Thou hast hid metals: man may take them thence;
But at his perill: when he digs the place,
He makes a grave; as if the thing had sense,
And threatned man, that he should fill the space.

Ev'n poysons praise thee. Should a thing be lost?
Should creatures want for want of heed their due?
Since where are poysons, antidotes are most:
The help stands close, and keeps the fear in view.

The sea, which seems to stop the traveller,
Is by a ship the speedier passage made.
The windes, who think they rule the mariner,
Are rul'd by him, and taught to serve his trade.

And as thy house is full, so I adore
Thy curious art in marshalling thy goods.
The hills with health abound; the vales with store;
The South with marble; North with furres & woods.

Hard things are glorious; easie things good cheap.
The common all men have; that which is rare
Men therefore seek to have, and care to keep.
The healthy frosts with summer-fruits compare.

Light without winde is glasse: warm without weight
Is wooll and furre: cool without closenesse, shade:
Speed without pains, a horse: tall without height,
A servile hawk: low without losse, a spade.

All countreys have enough to serve their need:
If they seek fine things, thou dost make them run
For their offence; and then dost turn their speed
To be commerce and trade from sunne to sunne.

Nothing wears clothes, but Man; nothing doth need
But he to wear them. Nothing useth fire,
But Man alone, to show his heav'nly breed:
And onely he hath fuell in desire.

When th' earth was dry, thou mad'st a sea of wet:
When that lay gather'd, thou didst broach the mountains:
When yet some places could no moisture get,
The windes grew gard'ners, and the clouds good fountains.

Rain, do not hurt my flowers; but gently spend
Your hony drops: presse not to smell them here:
When they are ripe, their odour will ascend,
And at your lodging with their thanks appeare.

How harsh are thorns to pears! and yet they make
A better hedge, and need lesse reparation.
How smooth are silks compared with a stake,
Or with a stone! yet make no good foundation.

Sometimes thou dost divide thy gifts to man,
Sometimes unite. The Indian nut alone
Is clothing, meat and trencher, drink and can,
Boat, cable, sail and needle, all in one.

Most herbs that grow in brooks, are hot and dry.
Cold fruits warm kernells help against the winde.
The lemmons juice and rinde cure mutually.
The whey of milk doth loose, the milk doth binde.

Thy creatures leap not, but expresse a feast,
Where all the guests sit close, and nothing wants.
Frogs marry fish and flesh; bats, bird and beast;
Sponges, non-sense and sense; mines, th' earth & plants.

To show thou art not bound, as if thy lot
Were worse then ours, sometimes thou shiftest hands.
Most things move th' under-jaw; the Crocodile not.
Most things sleep lying; th' Elephant leans or stands.

But who hath praise enough? nay, who hath any?
None can expresse thy works, but he that knows them:
And none can know thy works, which are so many,
And so complete, but onely he that owes them.

All things that are, though they have sev'rall wayes,
Yet in their being joyn with one advise
To honour thee: and so I give thee praise
In all my other hymnes, but in this twice.

Each thing that is, although in use and name
It go for one, hath many wayes in store
To honour thee; and so each hymne thy fame
Extolleth many wayes, yet this one more.

Hope

I gave to Hope a watch of mine: but he
           An anchor gave to me.
Then an old prayer-book I did present:
           And he an optick sent.
With that I gave a viall full of tears:
           But he a few green eares.
Ah Loyterer! I'le no more, no more I'le bring:
           I did expect a ring.

Sinnes round

Sorrie I am, my God, sorrie I am,
That my offences course it in a ring.
My thoughts are working like a busie flame,
Untill their cockatrice they hatch and bring:
And when they once have perfected their draughts,
My words take fire from my inflamed thoughts.

My words take fire from my inflamed thoughts,
Which spit it forth like the Sicilian Hill.
They vent the wares, and passe them with their faults,
And by their breathing ventilate the ill.
But words suffice not, where are lewd intentions:
My hands do joyn to finish the inventions.

My hands do joyn to finish the inventions:
And so my sinnes ascend three stories high,
As Babel grew, before there were dissensions.
Yet ill deeds loyter not: for they supplie
New thoughts of sinning: wherefore, to my shame,
Sorrie I am, my God, sorrie I am.

Gratefulnesse

Thou that hast giv'n so much to me,
Give one thing more, a gratefull heart.
See how thy beggar works on thee
             By art.

He makes thy gifts occasion more,
And sayes, If he in this be crost,
All thou hast giv'n him heretofore
             Is lost.

But thou didst reckon, when at first
Thy word our hearts and hands did crave,
What it would come to at the worst
             To save.

Perpetuall knockings at thy doore,
Tears sullying thy transparent rooms,
Gift upon gift, much would have more,
             And comes.

This notwithstanding, thou wentst on,
And didst allow us all our noise:
Nay, thou hast made a sigh and grone
             Thy joyes.

Not that thou hast not still above
Much better tunes, then grones can make;
But that these countrey-aires thy love
             Did take.

Wherefore I crie, and crie again;
And in no quiet canst thou be,
Till I a thankfull heart obtain
             Of thee:

Not thankfull, when it pleaseth me;
As if thy blessings had spare dayes:
But such a heart, whose pulse may be
                              Thy praise.

Giddinesse

Oh, what a thing is man! how farre from power,
　　From setled peace and rest!
He is some twentie sev'rall men at least
　　Each sev'rall houre.

One while he counts of heav'n, as of his treasure:
　　But then a thought creeps in,
And calls him coward, who for fear of sinne
　　Will lose a pleasure.

Now he will fight it out, and to the warres;
　　Now eat his bread in peace,
And snudge in quiet: now he scorns increase;
　　Now all day spares.

He builds a house, which quickly down must go,
　　As if a whirlwinde blew
And crusht the building: and it's partly true,
　　His minde is so.

O what a sight were Man, if his attires
　　Did alter with his minde;
And like a Dolphins skinne, his clothes combin'd
　　With his desires!

Surely if each one saw anothers heart,
　　There would be no commerce,
No sale or bargain passe: all would disperse,
　　And live apart.

Lord, mend or rather make us: one creation
　　Will not suffice our turn:
Except thou make us dayly, we shall spurn
　　Our own salvation.

Love unknown

Deare Friend, sit down, the tale is long and sad:
And in my faintings I presume your love
Will more complie then help. A Lord I had,
And have, of whom some grounds, which may improve,
I hold for two lives, and both lives in me.
To him I brought a dish of fruit one day,
And in the middle plac'd my heart. But he
                            (I sigh to say)
Lookt on a servant, who did know his eye
Better then you know me, or (which is one)
Then I my self. The servant instantly
Quitting the fruit, seiz'd on my heart alone,
And threw it in a font, wherein did fall
A stream of bloud, which issu'd from the side
Of a great rock: I well remember all,
And have good cause: there it was dipt and dy'd,
And washt, and wrung: the very wringing yet
Enforceth tears. *Your heart was foul, I fear.*
Indeed 'tis true. I did and do commit
Many a fault more then my lease will bear;
Yet still askt pardon, and was not deni'd.
But you shall heare. After my heart was well,
And clean and fair, as I one even-tide
                            (I sigh to tell)
Walkt by my self abroad, I saw a large
And spacious fornace flaming, and thereon
A boyling caldron, round about whose verge
Was in great letters set *AFFLICTION*.
The greatnesse shew'd the owner. So I went
To fetch a sacrifice out of my fold,
Thinking with that, which I did thus present,
To warm his love, which I did fear grew cold.
But as my heart did tender it, the man,

Who was to take it from me, slipt his hand,
And threw my heart into the scalding pan;
My heart, that brought it (do you understand?)
The offerers heart. *Your heart was hard, I fear.*
Indeed 'tis true. I found a callous matter
Began to spread and to expatiate there:
But with a richer drug then scalding water
I bath'd it often, ev'n with holy bloud,
Which at a board, while many drunk bare wine,
A friend did steal into my cup for good,
Ev'n taken inwardly, and most divine
To supple hardnesses. But at the length
Out of the caldron getting, soon I fled
Unto my house, where to repair the strength
Which I had lost, I hasted to my bed.
But when I thought to sleep out all these faults
                              (I sigh to speak)
I found that some had stuff'd the bed with thoughts,
I would say *thorns*. Deare, could my heart not break,
When with my pleasures ev'n my rest was gone?
Full well I understood, who had been there:
For I had giv'n the key to none, but one:
It must be he. *Your heart was dull, I fear.*
Indeed a slack and sleepie state of minde
Did oft possesse me, so that when I pray'd,
Though my lips went, my heart did stay behinde.
But all my scores were by another paid,
Who took the debt upon him. *Truly, Friend,*
For ought I heare, your Master shows to you
More favour then you wot of. Mark the end.
The Font did onely, what was old, renew:
The Caldron suppled, what was grown too hard:
The Thorns did quicken, what was grown too dull:
All did but strive to mend, what you had marr'd.
Wherefore be cheer'd, and praise him to the full
Each day, each houre, each moment of the week,
Who fain would have you be new, tender, quick.

Mans medley

Heark, how the birds do sing,
        And woods do ring.
All creatures have their joy: and man hath his.
    Yet if we rightly measure,
        Mans joy and pleasure
Rather hereafter, then in present, is.

To this life things of sense
        Make their pretence:
In th' other Angels have a right by birth:
    Man ties them both alone,
        And makes them one,
With th' one hand touching heav'n, with th' other earth.

In soul he mounts and flies,
        In flesh he dies.
He wears a stuffe whose thread is course and round,
    But trimm'd with curious lace,
        And should take place
After the trimming, not the stuffe and ground.

Not that he may not here
        Taste of the cheer,
But as birds drink, and straight lift up their head,
    So he must sip and think
        Of better drink
He may attain to, after he is dead.

But as his joyes are double;
        So is his trouble.
He hath two winters, other things but one:
    Both frosts and thoughts do nip,
        And bite his lip;
And he of all things fears two deaths alone.

Yet ev'n the greatest griefs
       May be reliefs,
Could he but take them right, and in their wayes.
    Happie is he, whose heart
        Hath found the art
To turn his double pains to double praise.

The Storm

If as the windes and waters here below
                    Do flie and flow,
My sighs and tears as busie were above;
                    Sure they would move
And much affect thee, as tempestuous times
Amaze poore mortals, and object their crimes.

Starres have their storms, ev'n in a high degree,
                    As well as we.
A throbbing conscience spurred by remorse
                    Hath a strange force:
It quits the earth, and mounting more and more
Dares to assault thee, and besiege thy doore.

There it stands knocking, to thy musicks wrong,
                    And drowns the song.
Glorie and honour are set by, till it
                    An answer get.
Poets have wrong'd poore storms: such dayes are best;
They purge the aire without, within the breast.

The Size

Content thee, greedie heart.
    Modest and moderate joyes to those, that have
Title to more hereafter when they part,
        Are passing brave.
    Let th' upper springs into the low
    Descend and fall, and thou dost flow.

    What though some have a fraught
Of cloves and nutmegs, and in cinamon sail;
If thou hast wherewithall to spice a draught,
        When griefs prevail;
    And for the future time art heir
    To th' Isle of spices, is 't not fair?

    To be in both worlds full
Is more then God was, who was hungrie here.
Wouldst thou his laws of fasting disanull?
        Enact good cheer?
    Lay out thy joy, yet hope to save it?
    Wouldst thou both eat thy cake, and have it?

    Great joyes are all at once;
But little do reserve themselves for more:
Those have their hopes; these what they have renounce,
        And live on score:
    Those are at home; these journey still,
    And meet the rest on Sions hill.

    Thy Saviour sentenc'd joy,
And in the flesh condemn'd it as unfit,
At least in lump: for such doth oft destroy;
        Whereas a bit
    Doth tice us on to hopes of more,
    And for the present health restore.

A Christians state and case
Is not a corpulent, but a thinne and spare,
Yet active strength: whose long and bonie face
                    Content and care
        Do seem to equally divide,
        Like a pretender, not a bride.

        Wherefore sit down, good heart;
Grasp not at much, for fear thou losest all.
If comforts fell according to desert,
        They would great frosts and snows destroy:
        For we should count, Since the last joy.

        Then close again the seam,
Which thou hast open'd: do not spread thy robe
In hope of great things. Call to minde thy dream,
                    An earthly globe,
        On whose meridian was engraven,
        These seas are tears, and heav'n the haven.

Complaining

Do not beguile my heart,
              Because thou art
My power and wisdome. Put me not to shame,
              Because I am
Thy clay that weeps, thy dust that calls.

Thou art the Lord of glorie;
              The deed and storie
Are both thy due: but I a silly flie,
              That live or die
According as the weather falls.

Art thou all justice, Lord?
              Shows not thy word
More attributes? Am I all throat or eye,
              To weep or crie?
Have I no parts but those of grief?

Let not thy wrathfull power
              Afflict my houre,
My inch of life: or let thy gracious power
              Contract my houre,
That I may climbe and finde relief.

Longing

      With sick and famisht eyes,
With doubling knees and weary bones,
          To thee my cries,
          To thee my grones,
To thee my sighs, my tears ascend:
               No end?

      My throat, my soul is hoarse;
My heart is wither'd like a ground
          Which thou dost curse.
          My thoughts turn round,
And make me giddie; Lord, I fall,
               Yet call.

      From thee all pitie flows.
Mothers are kinde, because thou art,
          And dost dispose
          To them a part:
Their infants, them; and they suck thee
             More free.

      Bowels of pitie, heare!
Lord of my soul, love of my minde,
          Bow down thine eare!
          Let not the winde
Scatter my words, and in the same
             Thy name!

      Look on my sorrows round!
Mark well my furnace! O what flames,
          What heats abound!
          What griefs, what shames!
Consider, Lord; Lord, bow thine eare,
            And heare!

Lord Jesu, thou didst bow
Thy dying head upon the tree:
　　　　　O be not now
　　　　　More dead to me!
Lord heare! *Shall he that made the eare,*
　　　　　　　Not heare?

　　　Behold, thy dust doth stirre,
It moves, it creeps, it aims at thee:
　　　　　Wilt thou deferre
　　　　　To succour me,
Thy pile of dust, wherein each crumme
　　　　　　Sayes, Come?

　　　To thee help appertains.
Hast thou left all things to their course,
　　　　　And laid the reins
　　　　　Upon the horse?
Is all lockt? hath a sinners plea
　　　　　　No key?

　　　Indeed the world's thy book,
Where all things have their leafe assign'd:
　　　　　Yet a meek look
　　　　　Hath interlin'd.
Thy board is full, yet humble guests
　　　　　　Finde nests.

　　　Thou tarriest, while I die,
And fall to nothing: thou dost reigne,
　　　　　And rule on high,
　　　　　While I remain
In bitter grief: yet am I stil'd
　　　　　　Thy childe.

　　　Lord, didst thou leave thy throne,
Not to relieve? how can it be,
　　　　　That thou art grown

Thus hard to me?
Were sinne alive, good cause there were
                    To bear.

            But now both sinne is dead,
And all thy promises live and bide.
                    That wants his head;
                    These speak and chide,
And in thy bosome poure my tears,
                    As theirs.

            Lord JESU, heare my heart,
Which hath been broken now so long,
                    That ev'ry part
                    Hath got a tongue!
Thy beggars grow; rid them away
                    To day.

            My love, my sweetnesse, heare!
By these thy feet, at which my heart
                    Lies all the yeare,
                    Pluck out thy dart,
And heal my troubled breast which cryes,
                    Which dyes.

The Collar

I struck the board, and cry'd, No more.
                     I will abroad.
     What? shall I ever sigh and pine?
My lines and life are free; free as the rode,
       Loose as the winde, as large as store.
          Shall I be still in suit?
      Have I no harvest but a thorn
      To let me bloud, and not restore
What I have lost with cordiall fruit?
                 Sure there was wine
Before my sighs did drie it: there was corn
          Before my tears did drown it.
       Is the yeare onely lost to me?
           Have I no bayes to crown it?
No flowers, no garlands gay? all blasted?
          All wasted?
    Not so, my heart: but there is fruit,
            And thou hast hands.
    Recover all thy sigh-blown age
On double pleasures: leave thy cold dispute
Of what is fit, and not. Forsake thy cage,
          Thy rope of sands,
Which pettie thoughts have made, and made to thee
     Good cable, to enforce and draw,
          And be thy law,
    While thou didst wink and wouldst not see.
          Away; take heed:
          I will abroad.
Call in thy deaths head there: tie up thy fears.
         He that forbears
       To suit and serve his need,
          Deserves his load.

But as I rav'd and grew more fierce and wilde
        At every word,
Me thoughts I heard one calling, *Child!*
        And I reply'd, *My Lord.*

The Glimpse

Whither away delight?
Thou cam'st but now; wilt thou so soon depart,
     And give me up to night?
For many weeks of lingring pain and smart
But one half houre of comfort to my heart?

     Me thinks delight should have
More skill in musick, and keep better time.
     Wert thou a winde or wave,
They quickly go and come with lesser crime:
Flowers look about, and die not in their prime.

     Thy short abode and stay
Feeds not, but addes to the desire of meat.
     Lime begg'd of old, they say,
A neighbour spring to cool his inward heat;
Which by the springs accesse grew much more great.

     In hope of thee my heart
Pickt here and there a crumme, and would not die;
     But constant to his part,
When as my fears foretold this, did replie,
A slender thread a gentle guest will tie.

     Yet if the heart that wept
Must let thee go, return when it doth knock.
     Although thy heap be kept
For future times, the droppings of the stock
May oft break forth, and never break the lock.

     If I have more to spinne,
The wheel shall go, so that thy stay be short.
     Thou knowst how grief and sinne
Disturb the work. O make me not their sport,
Who by thy coming may be made a court!

The Pulley

When God at first made man,
Having a glasse of blessings standing by,
Let us (said he) poure on him all we can:
Let the worlds riches, which dispersed lie,
Contract into a span.

So strength first made a way;
Then beautie flow'd, then wisdome, honour, pleasure:
When almost all was out, God made a stay,
Perceiving that alone of all his treasure
Rest in the bottome lay.

For if I should (said he)
Bestow this jewell also on my creature,
He would adore my gifts in stead of me,
And rest in Nature, not the God of Nature:
So both should losers be.

Yet let him keep the rest,
But keep them with repining restlesnesse:
Let him be rich and wearie, that at least,
If goodnesse leade him not, yet wearinesse
May tosse him to my breast.

The Flower

How fresh, O Lord, how sweet and clean
Are thy returns! ev'n as the flowers in spring;
    To which, besides their own demean,
The late-past frosts tributes of pleasure bring.
                Grief melts away
                Like snow in May,
    As if there were no such cold thing.

Who would have thought my shrivel'd heart
Could have recover'd greennesse? It was gone
    Quite under ground; as flowers depart
To see their mother-root, when they have blown;
                Where they together
                All the hard weather,
    Dead to the world, keep house unknown.

These are thy wonders, Lord of power,
Killing and quickning, bringing down to hell
    And up to heaven in an houre;
Making a chiming of a passing-bell.
                We say amisse,
                This or that is:
    Thy word is all, if we could spell.

O that I once past changing were,
Fast in thy Paradise, where no flower can wither!
    Many a spring I shoot up fair,
Offring at heav'n, growing and groning thither:
                Nor doth my flower
                Want a spring-showre,
    My sinnes and I joining together.

But while I grow in a straight line,
Still upwards bent, as if heav'n were mine own,
    Thy anger comes, and I decline:

What frost to that? what pole is not the zone,
              Where all things burn,
              When thou dost turn,
   And the least frown of thine is shown?

   And now in age I bud again,
After so many deaths I live and write;
   I once more smell the dew and rain,
And relish versing: O my onely light,
              It cannot be
              That I am he
   On whom thy tempests fell all night.

   These are thy wonders, Lord of love,
To make us see we are but flowers that glide:
   Which when we once can finde and prove,
Thou hast a garden for us, where to bide.
              Who would be more,
              Swelling through store,
   Forfeit their Paradise by their pride.

The Sonne

Let forrain nations of their language boast,
What fine varietie each tongue affords:
I like our language, as our men and coast:
Who cannot dresse it well, want wit, not words.
How neatly doe we give one onely name
To parents issue and the sunnes bright starre!
A sonne is light and fruit; a fruitfull flame
Chasing the fathers dimnesse, carri'd farre
From the first man in th' East, to fresh and new
Western discov'ries of posteritie.
So in one word our Lords humilitie
We turn upon him in a sense most true:
    For what Christ once in humblenesse began,
    We him in glorie call, *The Sonne of Man.*

Bitter-sweet

Ah my deare angrie Lord,
Since thou dost love, yet strike;
Cast down, yet help afford;
Sure I will do the like.

I will complain, yet praise;
I will bewail, approve:
And all my sowre-sweet dayes
I will lament, and love.

The Glance

When first thy sweet and gracious eye
Vouchsaf'd ev'n in the midst of youth and night
To look upon me, who before did lie
              Weltring in sinne;
  I felt a sugred strange delight,
Passing all cordials made by any art,
Bedew, embalme, and overrunne my heart,
            And take it in.

Since that time many a bitter storm
My soul hath felt, ev'n able to destroy,
Had the malicious and ill-meaning harm
            His swing and sway:
  But still thy sweet originall joy,
Sprung from thine eye, did work within my soul,
And surging griefs, when they grew bold, controll,
            And got the day.

If thy first glance so powerfull be,
A mirth but open'd and seal'd up again;
What wonders shall we feel, when we shall see
            Thy full-ey'd love!
  When thou shalt look us out of pain,
And one aspect of thine spend in delight
More then a thousand sunnes disburse in light,
            In heav'n above.

The Odour. 2. Cor. 2. 15

How sweetly doth *My Master* sound! *My Master*!
    As Amber-greese leaves a rich sent
        Unto the taster:
    So do these words a sweet content,
An orientall fragrancie, *My Master*.

With these all day I do perfume my minde,
    My minde ev'n thrust into them both:
        That I might finde
    What cordials make this curious broth,
This broth of smells, that feeds and fats my minde.

My Master, shall I speak? O that to thee
    My servant were a little so,
        As flesh may be;
    That these two words might creep & grow
To some degree of spicinesse to thee!

Then should the Pomander, which was before
    A speaking sweet, mend by reflection,
        And tell me more:
    For pardon of my imperfection
Would warm and work it sweeter then before.

For when *My Master*, which alone is sweet,
    And ev'n in my unworthinesse pleasing,
        Shall call and meet,
    My servant, as thee not displeasing,
That call is but the breathing of the sweet.

This breathing would with gains by sweetning me
    (As sweet things traffick when they meet)
        Return to thee.
    And so this new commerce and sweet
Should all my life employ and busie me.

The Rose

Presse me not to take more pleasure
       In this world of sugred lies,
And to use a larger measure
       Then my strict, yet welcome size.

First, there is no pleasure here:
       Colour'd griefs indeed there are,
Blushing woes, that look as cleare
       As if they could beautie spare.

Or if such deceits there be,
       Such delights I meant to say;
There are no such things to me,
       Who have pass'd my right away.

But I will not much oppose
       Unto what you now advise:
Onely take this gentle rose,
       And therein my answer lies.

What is fairer then a rose?
       What is sweeter? yet it purgeth.
Purgings enmitie disclose,
       Enmitie forbearance urgeth.

If then all that worldlings prize
       Be contracted to a rose;
Sweetly there indeed it lies,
       But it biteth in the close.

So this flower doth judge and sentence
       Worldly joyes to be a scourge:
For they all produce repentance,
       And repentance is a purge.

But I health, not physick choose:
      Onely though I you oppose,
Say that fairly I refuse,
      For my answer is a rose.

Discipline

Throw away thy rod,
Throw away thy wrath:
        O my God,
Take the gentle path.

For my hearts desire
Unto thine is bent:
        I aspire
To a full consent.

Not a word or look
I affect to own,
        But by book,
And thy book alone.

Though I fail, I weep:
Though I halt in pace,
        Yet I creep
To the throne of grace.

Then let wrath remove;
Love will do the deed:
        For with love
Stonie hearts will bleed.

Love is swift of foot;
Love 's a man of warre,
        And can shoot,
And can hit from farre.

Who can scape his bow?
That which wrought on thee,
        Brought thee low,
Needs must work on me.

Throw away thy rod;
Though man frailties hath,
      Thou art God:
Throw away thy wrath.

The Banquet

Welcome sweet and sacred cheer,
          Welcome deare;
With me, in me, live and dwell:
For thy neatnesse passeth sight,
          Thy delight
Passeth tongue to taste or tell.

O what sweetnesse from the bowl
          Fills my soul,
Such as is, and makes divine!
Is some starre (fled from the sphere)
          Melted there,
As we sugar melt in wine?

Or hath sweetnesse in the bread
          Made a head
To subdue the smell of sinne;
Flowers, and gummes, and powders giving
          All their living,
Lest the Enemy should winne?

Doubtlesse, neither starre nor flower
          Hath the power
Such a sweetnesse to impart:
Onely God, who gives perfumes,
          Flesh assumes,
And with it perfumes my heart.

But as Pomanders and wood
          Still are good,
Yet being bruis'd are better sented:
God, to show how farre his love
          Could improve,
Here, as broken, is presented.

When I had forgot my birth,
                    And on earth
In delights of earth was drown'd;
God took bloud, and needs would be
                    Spilt with me,
And so found me on the ground.

Having rais'd me to look up,
                    In a cup
Sweetly he doth meet my taste.
But I still being low and short,
                    Farre from court,
Wine becomes a wing at last.

For with it alone I flie
                    To the skie:
Where I wipe mine eyes, and see
What I seek, for what I sue;
                    Him I view,
Who hath done so much for me.

Let the wonder of his pitie
                    Be my dittie,
And take up my lines and life:
Hearken under pain of death,
                    Hands and breath;
Strive in this, and love the strife.

The Posie

Let wits contest,
And with their words and posies windows fill:
Lesse then the least
Of all thy mercies, is my posie still.

This on my ring,
This by my picture, in my book I write:
Whether I sing,
Or say, or dictate, this is my delight.

Invention rest,
Comparisons go play, wit use thy will:
Lesse then the least
Of all Gods mercies, is my posie still.

The Elixir

Teach me, my God and King,
    In all things thee to see,
And what I do in any thing,
    To do it as for thee:

Not rudely, as a beast,
    To runne into an action;
But still to make thee prepossest,
    And give it his perfection.

A man that looks on glasse,
    On it may stay his eye;
Or if he pleaseth, through it passe,
    And then the heav'n espie.

All may of thee partake:
    Nothing can be so mean,
Which with his tincture (for thy sake)
    Will not grow bright and clean.

A servant with this clause
    Makes drudgerie divine:
Who sweeps a room, as for thy laws,
    Makes that and th' action fine.

This is the famous stone
    That turneth all to gold:
For that which God doth touch and own
    Cannot for lesse be told.

Heaven

O who will show me those delights on high?
              Echo.   I.
Thou Echo, thou art mortall, all men know.
              Echo.   No.
Wert thou not born among the trees and leaves?
              Echo.   Leaves.
And are there any leaves, that still abide?
              Echo.   Bide.
What leaves are they? impart the matter wholly.
              Echo.   Holy.
Are holy leaves the Echo then of blisse?
              Echo.   Yes.
Then tell me, what is that supreme delight?
              Echo.   Light.
Light to the minde: what shall the will enjoy?
              Echo.   Joy.
But are there cares and businesse with the pleasure?
              Echo.   Leisure.
Light, joy, and leisure; but shall they persever?
              Echo.   Ever.

Love (III)

Love bade me welcome: yet my soul drew back,
                 Guiltie of dust and sinne.
But quick-ey'd Love, observing me grow slack
                 From my first entrance in,
Drew nearer to me, sweetly questioning,
                 If I lack'd any thing.

A guest, I answer'd, worthy to be here:
                 Love said, You shall be he.
I the unkinde, ungratefull? Ah my deare,
                 I cannot look on thee.
Love took my hand, and smiling did reply,
                 Who made the eyes but I?

Truth Lord, but I have marr'd them: let my shame
                 Go where it doth deserve.
And know you not, sayes Love, who bore the blame?
                 My deare, then I will serve.
You must sit down, sayes Love, and taste my meat:
                 So I did sit and eat.